The Nommo Gathering Black Writers Collective

300 PROMPTS FOR BLACK WRITERS

STEPHANIE GADLIN

ISBN: 9798672433226
www.nommowriters.org

Nommo's creative writing prompts are a fun and stress-free way to jump start your creative writing experience and get through writer's block.

Our prompts are created with Black writers in mind. Some are fun, some are silly, and some may be challenging. But all are designed to get you out of your head and writing. With just 15 minutes a day, you will develop writing discipline and work toward building a catalog of creativity that you can use later as a springboard to a new and wonderful work of literary art.

HOW TO USE NOMMO PROMPTS

- Grab a notebook and your favorite pen or pencil.
- Find a quiet and comfortable place to write.
- Set a timer for five minutes.
- Sit quietly, breathe deeply, and release the cares from your mind.
- Now set your timer for 10 minutes.
- Pick a random number between numbers 1 and 300.
- Start the timer, locate the prompt and start writing-- whatever comes to mind--uninterrupted. Just write, even if you're can only think of one word.
- Remember, there is no right or wrong. Just be free to create. No one has to read it and you don't have to share it with anyone.
- Vow to do this process all over again tomorrow.
- After one full week of writing prompts spend 30 minutes reading your entries aloud. Determine if there's a spark for your next literary project.

NOMMO
PROMPTS

1.BLACK IS BEAUTIFUL
2.WHAT IS THE PURPOSE OF MELANIN?
3.DESCRIBE A DREAM
4.MICHAEL JACKSON'S SONG "BEAT IT" IS ON THE RADIO

5. WHAT DOES IT MEAN TO BE BLACK?

6. WRITE ABOUT YOUR FAVORITE CHILDHOOD MEMORY

7. GRACE JONES IS SEATED NEXT TO YOU ON AN AIRPLANE

8. JOHN SHAFT AND FOXY BROWN GET MARRIED; WRITE THEIR WEDDING VOWS

9. WHAT HAPPENED WHEN YOU GOT A REPARATIONS CHECK?

10. WHAT IS THE FUNNIEST JOKE YOU HAVE EVER HEARD?

11. WRITE A SCENE INVOLVING A WARRIOR AND A LION

12. WHAT DOES FREEDOM MEAN TO YOU?

13. CREATE A CONSPIRACY THEORY

14. DESCRIBE A TODDLER TRYING TO GET THE ATTENTION OF A PARENT

15. YOU ARE VISITING EGYPT FOR THE FIRST TIME, DESCRIBE THE EXPERIENCE.

16. YOU GO TO A STRIP CLUB AND SEE YOUR DAUGHTER ON STAGE

17. WHAT IS YOUR FAVORITE MOVIE?

18. WRITE A LETTER FROM A PRISON INMATE TO A FATHER

19. DESCRIBE YOUR BEST VACATION

20. YOUR LIP-GLOSS IS POPPIN'

21.WHO IS YOUR HERO?

22.TOO BLESSED TO BE STRESSED

23.DESCRIBE YOUR FAVORITE OUTFIT

24.YOU HEAR SOMEONE BANGING ON THEDOOR

25. DESCRIBE FIVE DANCES IN A SOUL TRAIN LINE

26. YOU HAVE JUST BEEN HIRED TO PROMOTE A VIOLENT GANGSTER RAP SINGLE

27. ADD A SCENE TO THE MOVIE, "THE COLOR PURPLE."

28. WRITE DIALOGUE BETWEEN BOOKER T. WASHINGTON AND W.E.B. DUBOIS

29.HE WORE A BLUE SUIT WITH A RED TIE
30.SHE HAD ON HIGH HEELS
31.WRITE A SHORT STORY ABOUT STAGECOACH MARY
32.ROBBING PETER TO PAY PAUL

33. BESSIE COLEMAN IS ABOUT TO TAKE FLIGHT

34. WRITE ABOUT A BAPTISM

35. B.B. KING IS ON STAGE

36. DESCRIBE A FEAST

37. BEAR WITNESS TO A HISTORICAL EVENT

38. AT FIRST, I THOUGHT IT WAS A JOKE

39. DESCRIBE A PARADE WITHOUT USING THE WORD "PARADE"

40. WRITE ABOUT FIRST, TIME TEENAGE PARENTS

41.CREATE A NEW GOVERNMENT AGENCY

42.WRITE A CONVERSATION BETWEEN MICHAEL JORDAN AND KOBE BRYANT

43.WRITE A SHORT STORY ABOUT COOKING COLLARD GREENS

44.YOU ARE ASKED TO GIVE A SPEECH BEFORE THE UNITED NATIONS

45. THE NATIONAL GUARD HAS BEEN CALLED

46. THE PRESS AND COMB

47. DESCRIBE THE EXPERIENCE OF A SUBSTITUTE TEACHER

48. WHY SHOULD WE CARE ABOUT EVENTS IN OTHER PARTS OF THE WORLD?

49. THE DEFENDANT ENTERED A COURTROOM

50. WRITE A LETTER TO YOUR NEWSPAPER

51. WRITE A BELIEVABLE FAKE NEWS STORY

52. WRITE A POEM ABOUT LOVE

53. HOW DO YOU FEEL ABOUT VALENTINE'S DAY?

54. HOW FAR BACK CAN YOU TRACE YOUR FAMILY TREE?

55. DESCRIBE AN ORANGE WITHOUT USING THE WORD ORANGE.

56. AS SUPREME RULER, YOU CAST YOUR FIRST DECREE

57.YOU ARE RIDING A GREYHOUND BUS

58.I BROUGHT YOU IN THIS WORLD. DON'T MAKE ME TAKE YOU OUT.

59.HE WENT TO THE MAILBOX

60.IT IS THE 1970S AND YOU WORK AT THE POST OFFICE

61. AND THEN MAHALIA SANG

62. DESCRIBE A CRAB BOIL

63. CHITTERLINGS ARE ON THE STOVE

64. YOU ARE THE LAST BLACK PERSON ON EARTH

65.WRITE A CONVERSATION BETWEEN JAMES BROWN AND FREDERICK DOUGLASS

66.HE ASKED ME TO DANCE

67.TO BE YOUNG, GIFTED, AND BLACK

68.WRITE A MONOLOGUE FOR BOO THE FOOL

69. WRITE A CONVERSATION BETWEEN A GANG BANGER AND A MAYOR

70. CONVINCE THE GOVERNOR WE STILL NEED LIBRARIES

71. SOMEONE YELLS THE WORD "NIGGER" FROM A PASSING AUTOMOBILE

72. WHAT MUSIC INSPIRES YOU?

73.DESCRIBE YOUR FIRST CRUSH.

74.WRITE A SERMON TO BE DELIVERED BEFORE ATHEISTS

75.PRESIDENT OBAMA'S LEGACY

76.THE BARBERSHOP WAS CROWDED

77. WHAT DO WE OWE VETERANS

78. WHAT IS SOUL MUSIC

79. YOU ARE DRIVING AT NIGHT AND THE POLICE PULL YOU OVER

80. WHO IS YOUR FAVORITE COUSIN?

81.DESCRIBE A HAUNTED HOUSE

82.WRITE A CONVERSATION IN EBONICS

83.SHOW A CHARACTER MAKING ICE CREAM

84.DESCRIBE A MEAN BABYSITTER

86.DINA ROSS AND THE SUPREMES

87.YOU LOOK OUT THE WINDOW AND SEE SOMETHING YOU CANNOT BELIEVE

88.YOU SEE A CONFEDERATE FLAG

89.JACK JOHNSON HAS JUST WON THE HEAVYWEIGHT TITLE

90.THE FIRST BOOK I READ FROM START TO FINISH

91.YOUR DATE SAYS, "I DON'T EAT PORK" AND YOU MADE HAM

92.YOU OWN A JUKE JOINT; DESCRIBE THREE CUSTOMERS

93. DO THE TWIST

94. INCLUDE THE PHRASE, "THE LONE RANGER WAS BLACK"

95. DESCRIBE THE MOMENT GEORGE CARVER PICKED UP A PEANUT

96. EXPLAIN RACISM TO A BEING FROM ANOTHER UNIVERSE

98.A COMPUTER AND A PRINTER

100.DESCRIBE AN INHUMANMONSTER

101.BLACK DON'T CRACK
102.QUEEN LATIFAH
103.SAM COOKE'S VOICE WAS LIKE
104.DESCRIBE A SURPRISE PARTY

105.YOU ARE A SUPERHERO
106.DESCRIBE THE AGING PROCESS
107.GUN VIOLENCE
108.HE PREACHED A SERMON

109.SHE WORE A RED DRESS
110.SHE IS A FAST WOMAN
111.AND THEN THE CHOIR STOOD UP
112.WE DECIDED TO MAKE GUMBO

113. AND THEN I SAW A DOG
114. YOU ARE WALKING TO THE STORE
115. WHO MADE THE POTATO SALAD?
116. BEYONCÉ AND HARRIET TUBMAN

117.THE LAST WHITE MAN ON EARTH
118.BLACK WOMEN ARE
119.BLACK MEN ARE
120.BLACK YOUTH ARE

121.IF YOU COULD PASS FOR WHITE
122.YOU HAVE JUST ARRIVED IN HAITI
123.FOUR CHILDREN ARE PLAYING
124.IF YOU HAD ONE WISH

125.YOUR FAVORITE HOLIDAY
126.EAT YOUR VEGETABLES
127.TWO COWBOYS SHARE TIPS
128."BLACK LIVES MATTER!"

129.A POT OF HAM HOCKS COOKING

130.A MAD SCIENTIST'S INVENTION

131.ROSA PARKS

132.A WORLD WITHOUT WHITE PEOPLE

133.DESCRIBE GOING TO THE CIRCUS

134.SHE SAID SHE WAS FROM GABON

135.TOMORROW I WILL

136.IT WAS STARTING TO RAIN

141.MAKE UP A NEW VOODOO RITUAL

142.SHE DROVE A BMW

143.INTEGRATION OR SEPARATION

144.THE CONDO LOOKED LIKE

145.THEY WERE SO POOR
146.WHITE CASTLE HAMBURGER
147.WHAT IS HERITAGE
148.DESCRIBE A FAMILY

149. THE RAP CONCERT JUST STARTED

150. A SCENE FROM GOOD TIMES

151. WRITE AN ACCEPTANCE SPEECH

152. SIDNEY POITIER

153.HALLE BERRY
154.THE QUEEN IS HERE
155.PRISON INDUSTRIAL COMPLEX
156.WRITE ABOUT A FAMILY REUNION

157. A PET GIRAFFE

158. WRITE A HAIKU

159. WRITE ABOUT A FUNERAL SERVICE

160. INVENT A PLANET

164.SHOULD VOTING BE MANDATORY

165.WRITE ABOUT A BABY SHOWER

166.I AM VEGAN

167.THE CREDIT CARD WAS DECLINED

168.WRITE A RESIGNATION LETTER

169.CIGAR SMOKE
170.DESCRIBE AN INSANE ASYLUM
171.IF I WERE AN ANIMAL
172.DESCRIBE A CAR ACCIDENT

173.BILL COSBY

174.DESCRIBE CHILDBIRTH

175.CREATE AN INVENTION

176.WHAT ARE YOU GRATEFUL FOR?

177.GOD IS
178.A PROSTITUTE IN CHURCH
179.HE WAS LIGHT SKIN
180.SHE WAS THE COLOR OF

181. THE BLACK PANTHER PARTY

182. YOUR FAVORITE TEACHER

183. A TUSKEGEE AIRMAN SPEAKS

184. A COSPLAY CONVENTION

189. EMANCIPATION PROCLAMATION
190. A MESSAGE IN A BOTTLE
191. YOU GOT MCDONALD'S MONEY?
192. THE RESTAURANT IS CLOSED

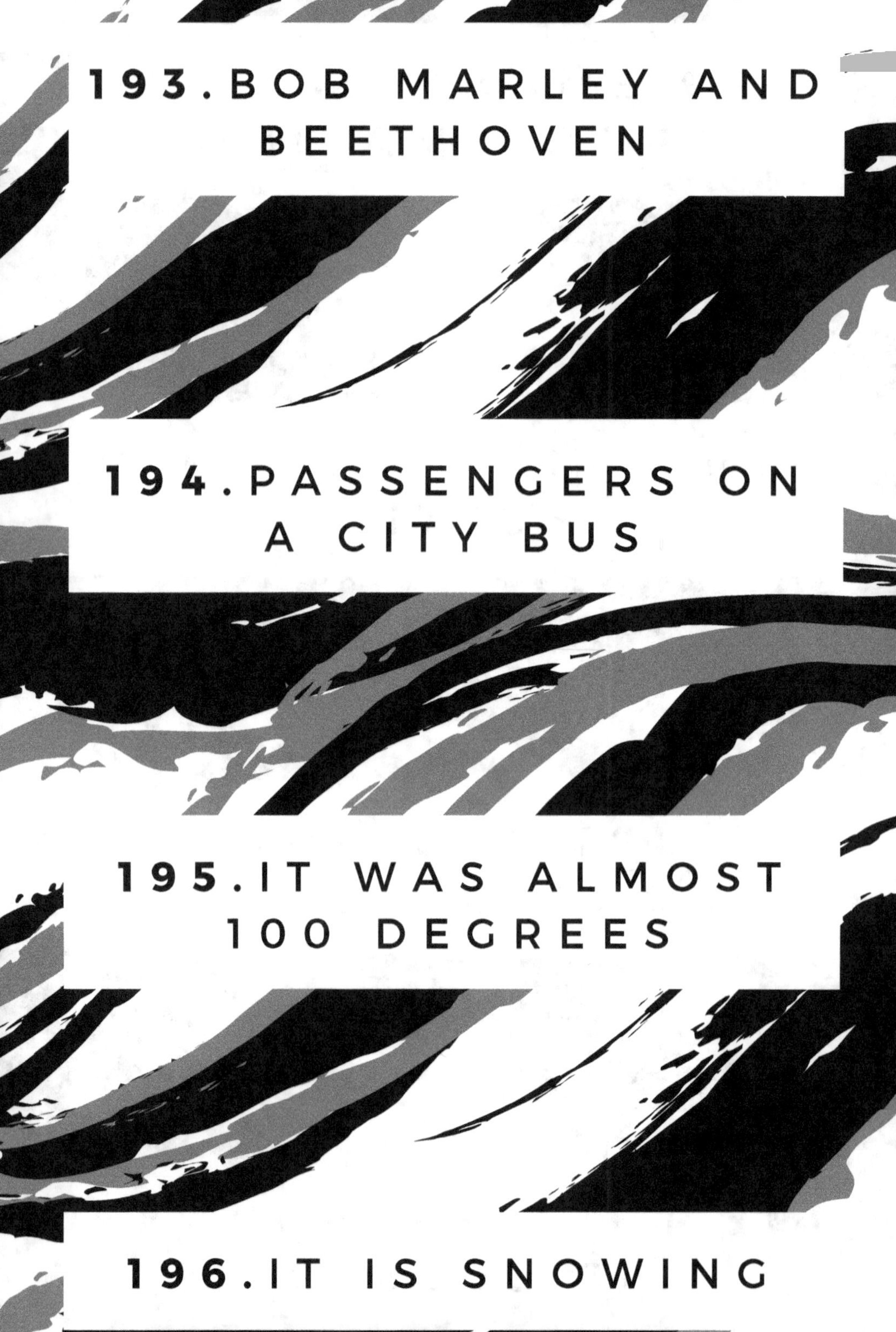

193.BOB MARLEY AND BEETHOVEN
194.PASSENGERS ON A CITY BUS
195.IT WAS ALMOST 100 DEGREES
196.IT IS SNOWING

197.CAN BLACK CULTURE BE STOLEN

198.YOU MANAGE A GROCERY STORE

199.YOU ARE A POLICE OFFICER

200.THE ONLY BLACK AT YOUR JOB

201.YOUR DOORBELL RANG
202.BLACK EYE PEAS
203.TRAVELLING THROUGH MEXICO
204.THE DENTIST LOOKED LIKE

205.WHO DO YOU ADMIRE?

206.WHO DO YOU DESPISE?

207.A BANK ROBBERY IN PLACE

208.MILES DAVIS' HORN

209. ARETHA FRANKLIN WAS

210. MEAN TEXT MESSAGES

211. IT IS 100 YEARS IN THE FUTURE

212. THE STREETLIGHTS CAME ON

213.THE FIRST BLACK MAN ON MARS
214.DESCRIBE YOUR DREAM HOUSE
215.DESCRIBE YOUR DREAM CAR
216.YOU OWE $200 IN RENT

221.DR. KING AND MALCOLM X

222.PRINCE

223.SHE WANTED A NOSE JOB

224.SOUL FOOD

227.WHAT IS AFRICA TO ME?

228.IS AMERICA FOR EVERYBODY?

229.SAMMY DAVIS JR.

230.TELL A SHORT BEDTIME STORY

231.WHAT SCARES YOU?

232.A BLACK VAMPIRE

233.RICHARD PRYOR
234.WHITNEY HOUSTON
235.A CAT
236.AN AFRICAN KING

237.DO NOT WORRY

238.BLACK HISTORY MONTH

239.FRESH BAKED COOKIES

240.THE BATTLE OF THE BANDS

241.WRITE A LETTER TO YOURSELF

242.INVENT A PIRATE LANGUAGE

243.THE HOLY QURAN

244.I GOT SOUL

245.DESCRIBE AN ELDER
246.CHRISTMAS
247.REALITY TV
248.ROOTS, THE TV MINISERIES

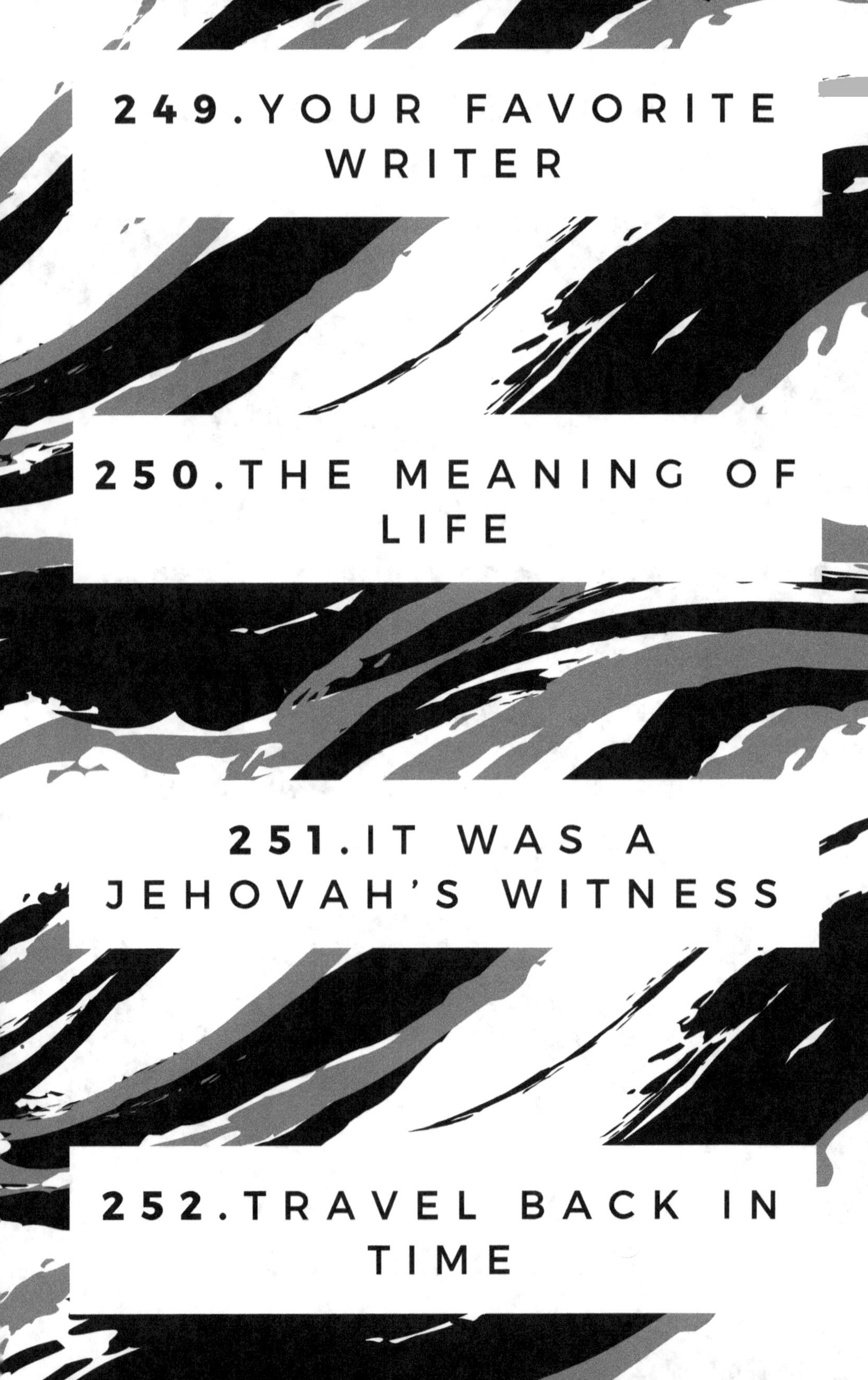

249. YOUR FAVORITE WRITER

250. THE MEANING OF LIFE

251. IT WAS A JEHOVAH'S WITNESS

252. TRAVEL BACK IN TIME

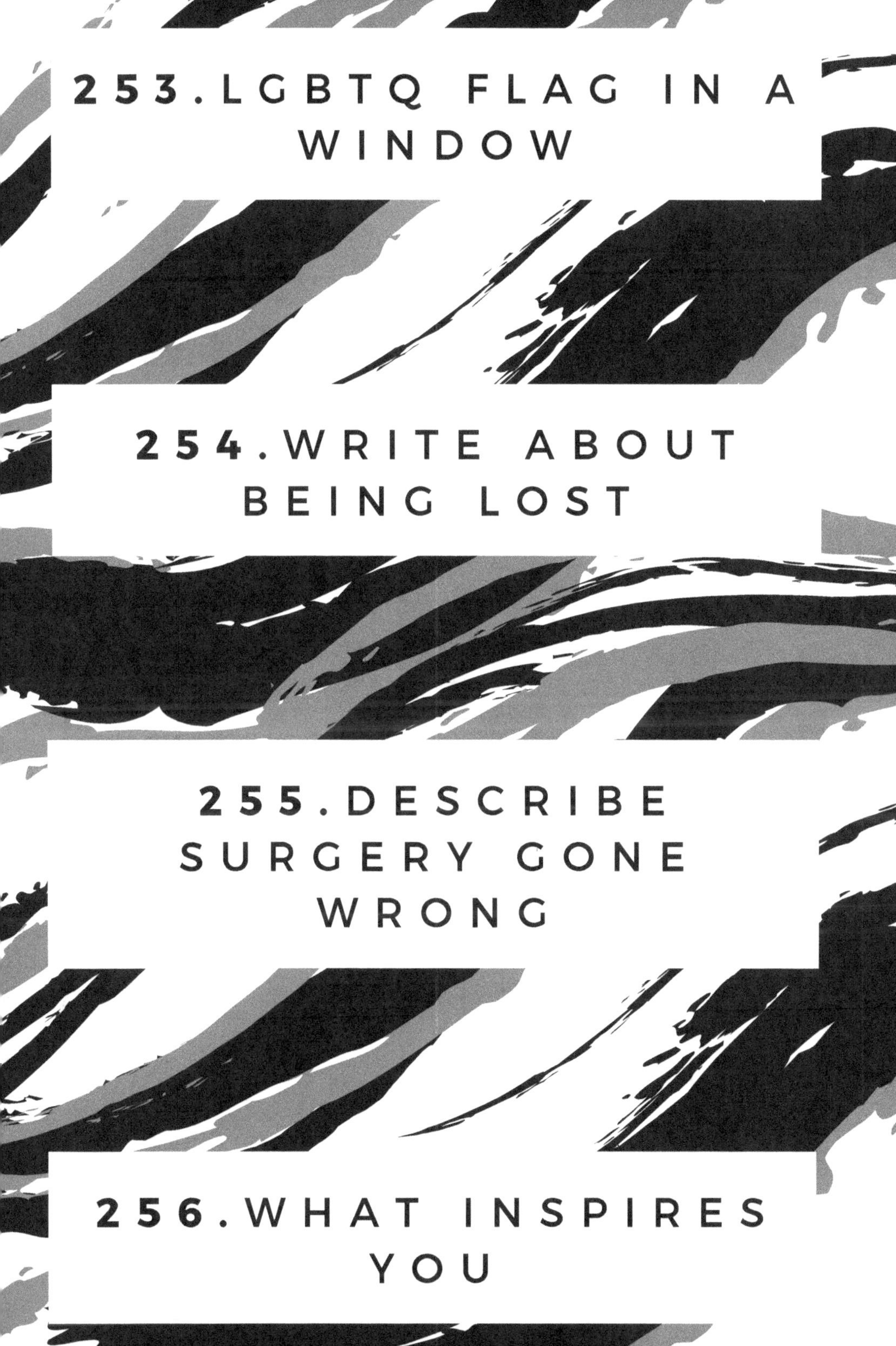

253.LGBTQ FLAG IN A WINDOW
254.WRITE ABOUT BEING LOST
255.DESCRIBE SURGERY GONE WRONG
256.WHAT INSPIRES YOU

257.MUHAMMAD ALI
258.YOU ARE AT A PARK
259.THE ELECTRIC SLIDE
260.CLARENCE THOMAS

261.GREEN

262.DESCRIBE A PHYSICAL DISABILITY

263.BLUE

264.YOUR HIGH SCHOOL PROM

265.PINK
266.AQUA
267.WRITE ABOUT A CHOICE
268.ORANGE

269.WHEN SOMEONE DIES

270.DESCRIBE YOUR MORNING

271.YOU MANAGE A GROCERY STORE

272.DESCRIBE A POSTAL WORKER

273. A SON ANNOUNCES HE IS TRANS

274. A LYNCH ROPE AND A TREE

275. BLACK EYE PEAS

276. FIRST TIME DRIVER

277.THE BALLERINA LOOKED LIKE

278.LOOKING INTO A CRYSTAL BALL

279.WHO DO YOU ADMIRE?

280.PEOPLE IN THE PROJECTS

281. WHO DO YOU DESPISE?
282. YOU HIT THE LOTTO
283. NEPTUNE
284. ELDERBERRY SYRUP

285.ONIONS MAKE ME CRY
286.THE FIRST BLACK MAN ON MARS
287.DESCRIBE YOUR DREAM HOUSE
288.DESCRIBE YOUR DREAM CAR

289.YOU JUST FOUND $1,000,000
290.DESCRIBE A CIVIL RIGHTS PROTEST
291.WRITE ABOUT A FIRST DATE
292.SANDRA BLAND, GEORGE FLOYD

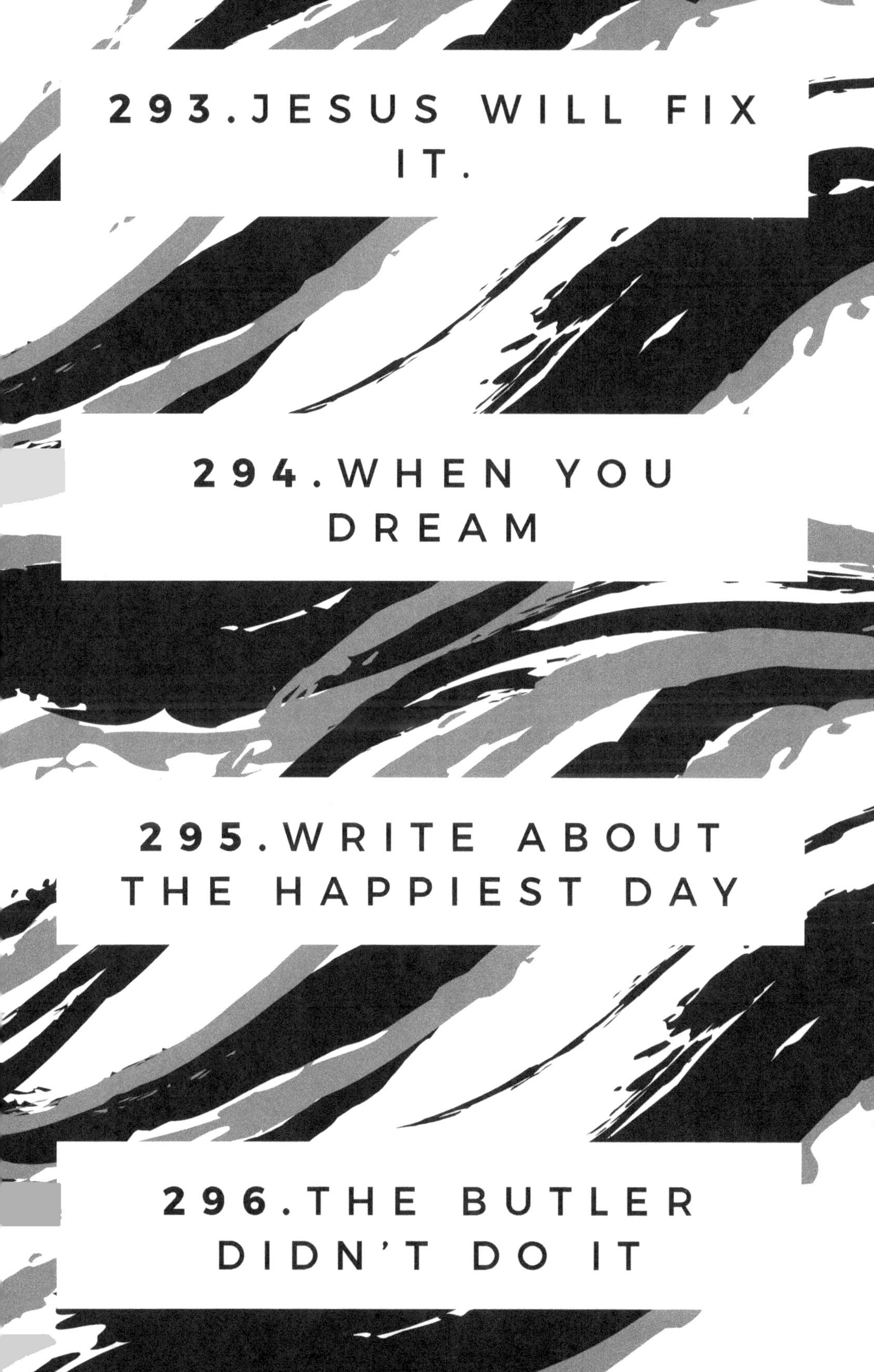

293.JESUS WILL FIX IT.
294.WHEN YOU DREAM
295.WRITE ABOUT THE HAPPIEST DAY
296.THE BUTLER DIDN'T DO IT

297.STAND BACK!

298.DESCRIBE A RUNWAY SHOW

299.I LOVE MYSELF

300.WE LIFT AS WE CLIMB